This book is dedicated to my beautiful mother. Without her unmatched creativity in the kitchen, I would not be the cook I am today.

Love you to the moon and back.

Image | Bri Ramos

NOT THE WORST COOKBOOK

30-ISH DELICIOUS RECIPES YOUR FAMILY DOESN'T DESERVE

1

ABOUT ME

First things first; I am *not* a chef.

I didn't go to culinary school and I've never worked in Food and Beverage. I am simply a teen mom who had a family of 5 to feed by 21 and figured shit out through trial, error, and expensive taste (buds).

I'm a good cook; not a *chef.*

What's the difference? I don't do gourmet or beautiful plating; I pull dinner out of my ass with whatever's in my kitchen after working all day with zero planning.

These recipes are a culmination of my grandmother and mom's cooking with a tight budget and deep love for food.

Yes, I had awesome women influence my cooking, but I didn't "know" how to cook heading into motherhood. If I can figure this shit out, you can too.

Sure, I've honed my skills over the fucking COUNTLESS meals I'm forced to provide my starving family, but that means you can too!

I'm incredibly proud of this book and can't thank you enough for your support! If you love it, tell your friends! If you don't, remember no one likes a narc.

SARA BUCKLEY
NOT THE WORST MOM

Image | Bri Ramos

CONTENTS

What to expect.

Image | Sara Buckley

Image | Bri Ramos

MY FAMILY IS MY LIFE AND I'D DO ANYTHING FOR THEM, BUT I SWEAR TO GOD WHEN I HAVE TO PUT DINNER AWAY AFTER COOKING IT, I WANT TO BURN THIS WHOLE FUCKING PLACE TO THE GROUND.

APPETIZERS

Pregame your food.

Image | Sara Buckley

Image | Sara Buckley

DON'T TOUCH YOUR GENITALS JALEPEÑO POPPERS

WARNING: This is one of those wear-gloves-don't-touch-your-eyes-or-genitals-or-someone-else's-genitals-for-awhile kind of recipes. Yes, I know from personal experience, thanks for asking. For the love of your own physical comfort, get some gloves to prep this. According to science, the wrinklier the pepper = the spicier. But according to my grandma, you literally never can tell so be careful. It's spicy roulette.

ACTIVE 30min **TOTAL** 1hr **SERVES** 6-8 Servings

INGREDIENTS

- *12 whole jalapenos, washed*
- *8 oz of plain cream cheese*
- *1 cup cheddar cheese (or monterrey, or colby - whatever)*
- *1/4-1/2 cup sliced scallions, depends on how much you like onions*
- *1 pound center cut bacon*
- *1-2 tablespoons garlic powder (who cares, just eyeball it)*
- *1 tsp salt*

1. Put on those goddamn gloves before you do anything.
2. WITH THE GLOVES ON, preheat the oven to 400°.
3. Cut the jalapenos lengthwise (I SWEAR TO GOD IF YOU AREN'T WEARING GLOVES...) and use a spoon to scrape out all the seeds and white veins. Juicer 'penos will literally pepper spray you in the open eyeballs so watch out for that shit.
4. Cut bacon in half.
5. Combine the cream cheese, cheddar cheese, scallions, garlic powder, and salt in a bowl.
6. Spoon mix into each jalapeno half, just to the top. Wrap each pepper with bacon, secure with toothpicks.
7. Cook on top baking rack for 25-30 minutes, until bacon is fully cooked.

ARTICHOKE ME DADDY DIP

I used to make this with spinach, but I'm telling you kale is SO much better. It holds a firmer texture after being baked and doesn't release as much water, but if you have a peasant's palate and love slimy greens, by all means use spinach.

ACTIVE 25 min **TOTAL** 1hr 10min **SERVES** 6-8 Servings

INGREDIENTS

- *1 bunch of kale*
- *13.75 ounce can of artichoke hearts, drained*
- *1 cup mayonaise (or veganaise)*
- *2-∞ garlic cloves*
- *1 cup grated parmesean cheese and some for the top*
- *black pepper*
- *chips or crackers*

GARNISH/PAIRING

bottle of champagne
entitlement

1. Preheat the oven to 350°.
2. Devein the kale (aka remove that thick ass, gross thing) and chop into 1"x1" pieces. I never measured that, i'm just guessing.
3. Sautee over medium heat with a LITTLE olive oil until wilted.
4. Drain and chop the artichoke hearts.
5. Combine kale, artichoke, mayo, parmesan, pepper and however much garlic your heart tells you.
6. Top with more parm if you please.
7. Bake for 20-25 minutes until the edges are bubbly and the top has browned.
8. Serve hot with chips, crackers, bread or whatever the fuck floats your boat.

Image | Sara Buckley

Image | Sara Buckley

BUCKLEY'S BRIE-LIEVE IT OR NOT

Do not let puff pastry intimidate you! It is a lot easier to work with than you think and the possibilities are endless. Having some fruit to shovel this molten goodness in your mouth won't only broaden the dish's palate, but it'll feel less like literally shoveling cheese wrapped in bread down your gullet.

ACTIVE 15 min **TOTAL** 50min **SERVES** 6-8 Servings

INGREDIENTS

- *1 sheet puff pastry, thawed*
- *1 wheel of brie cheese*
- *4 tbs of apricot preserves*
- *1/4 c slivered almonds, dry roasted*
- *1/2 c gorgonzola cheese crumbles*
- *1 egg, beaten*
- *flour, for dusting*

GARNISH/PAIRING

crackers
baguette slices
pears and/or apples

1. Preheat the oven to 400° and thaw puff pastry according to the packaging. Dust your workspace with flour, and lay the puff pastry out flat.
2. Dry roast the almonds in a pan over medium heat. Do not add oil or any non-stick spray. Move the almonds around the pan until they are golden brown. WATCH THEM CAREFULLY: these fuckers can burn quick.
3. Cut your wheel o' brie in half and place in the center of the puff pastry. Add a layer of gorgonzola and top with the other half of brie.
4. Spread your preserves over the top of the brie and sprinkle those toasty ass almonds on top!
5. Fold the puff pastry, overlapping to cover the entire wheel. If you have a lot of excess pastry, you can trim some off!
6. Brush the outside with the beaten egg.
7. Bake for 35-40 minutes until the puff pastry is golden brown and allow to cool for 10 minutes.
8. Serve hot with crackers, baguette, pears, apples, all of the above or eat it with a fucking fork because no one says you can't!

GRAPE TRUFFLESQUE

You are not ready for how good this shit tastes. I'm not kidding, it'll impress even the lowliest of food peasants. Unless you have some stupid aversion to one of these wonderful ingredients, don't knock it 'til you try it. These babies are the perfect holiday appetizer but I prefer them paired with a bottle of champagne all to myself while I binge filthy period pieces. You probably won't find crushed pistachios, so just buy whole, roasted and salted ones and crush them yourself.

ACTIVE 35 min **TOTAL** 35 min **SERVES** 1-2 depending on how selfish you are

INDGREDIENTS

- *red seedless grapes*
- *4 oz log of goat cheese*
- *crushed roasted, salted pistachios*

GARNISH/PAIRING

bottle of champagne
entitlement

1. Wash the grapes, duh.
2. Double bag the pistachios in gallon plastic baggies and take out all your rage with a meat mallot to crush these delicious fuckers.
3. Grab about a tablespoon-ish of goat cheese and mold around one grape. You want good cheese coverage, so add or subtract according to the size of the grape.
4. Roll in crushed pistachios. Serve immediately.

You can prep these the day before, but stop after the goat cheese and roll them in the pistachios just before serving. Only make what you think you'll need as these don't save TOO well because the pistachios get a bit soggy. I still eat them the next day though because these are my kryptonite.

Image | Sara Buckley

Image | Sara Buckley

BONUS RECIPE!

PREGNANT DATES

I've been married a long time, so I have no idea what it's like to date nowadays. However, any evening that begins or ends with getting stuffed like these dates would be a "win" in my book. You can use thin or thick cut bacon and even brush with a little maple syrup for extra sweetness.

ACTIVE 25 min **TOTAL** 55 min **SERVES** 6-8 Servings

INGREDIENTS

- *12 oz of medjool dates, pitted*
- *4 oz log of goat cheese*
- *1 lb of bacon, cut in half*
- *crushed roasted, salted pistachios*
- *toothpicks*

GARNISH/PAIRING

not a damn thing, baby girl

1. Preheat the oven to 350°. Slice the bacon in half. One piece of bacon will wrap two dates.
2. Use a spoon to fill each date with goat cheese and top with a generous sprinkle of pistachios.
3. Wrap each date with a bacon slice and secure with a toothpick. Put the bacon "seam" on the bottom and the open part of the date facing up so your shit doesn't fall apart.
4. Bake for about 12 minutes then rearrange if necessary or want to crisp the bacon to your liking and cook for an additional 10 minutes.
5. Let cool before serving because you know some idiot will bite into this delicious lava without hesitation.

HOW MANY TIMES CAN YOU SAY *FUCK* WHILE COOKING AND HAVE IT STILL BE "MADE WITH LOVE"?

Image | Bri Ramos

SOUP + SALAD

Eat it or go fuck yourself.

Image | Sara Buckley

GRANDMA ROSE'S FIDEO

Image | Sara Buckley

If you're looking for the exact recipe for the perfect bowl of fideo, you're in the wrong place. This is my great grandma's recipe that my grandma taught me how to make. I'll do my best to give you better measurements than she gave me, but if you still need help: figure it the fuck out. It's soup, not science.

ACTIVE 30 min **TOTAL** 55 min **SERVES** No fucking clue

INGREDIENTS

- *1 ounce package of fideo noodles (you can also hand break angel hair or spaghetti)*
- *Vegetable oil*
- *4 roma tomatoes*
- *1/2 medium yellow onion*
- *3 cloves of garlic*
- *6-8 cups of broth (add broth if you prefer it soupier)*
- *Salt and pepper*

GARNISH/PAIRING

lemon
hot sauce
a quesadilla

1. Bring a medium pot of water to a full boil with a dash of salt. Score each end of the tomatoes with an X. Once boiling, cook the tomatoes for 30-40 seconds. Remove and place in ice water. Once cooled to handle, remove the skins.

2. Heat a few tablespoons of oil over medium heat in that same pot after you're done with the tomatoes because we're not trying to dirty the whole goddamn kitchen.

3. Brown the noodles in oil until they reach a deep golden brown. DO NOT have your heat too high and keep turning because this will go from not done to BURNT real quick.

4. Blend the shit out of your naked tomatoes, onion, garlic and a cup of broth.

5. CAREFULLY add the mixture to the noodles. Turn your heat down and watch out for MAGMA shrapnel from the exploding tomato sauce.

6. Though blended, the tomato, garlic and onion are still raw. Cook on medium for, i'm thinking 8 minutes? I'll be honest, I 100% go by the smell here, so God speed with this step.

7. Once you're sure it's fully cooked, add the remaining broth and any additional seasonings if you'd like.

Thicker fideo (less broth) is great as a side along with rice and beans. Or you can make it soupier and eat with lemon and hot sauce. I also highly recommend dipping a quesadilla in it as well. It's like the Mexican version of tomato soup with a grilled cheese.

POZOLE RO-HOE

Pozole Rojo is my fucking jam. I didn't learn this one from grandma but by trial and error. It's great to warm the cold hearts of your offspring in the wintertime. Don't be intimidated by the extra steps. You can do this and will look like a culinary goddess!

ACTIVE 45 min **TOTAL** 1 hr 30 min **SERVES** 8-10

Image | Sara Buckley

INGREDIENTS

- *2 28 oz cans of hominy, drained and rinsed*
- *2 pounds of pork shoulder, cut into medium sized cubes*
- *2 onions*
- *6 guajillo chiles, cleaned*
- *1 bulb of garlic, plus a few loose cloves*
- *Oregano*
- *Cumin*
- *Bay Leaves*
- *Salt*
- *Pepper*

GARNISH/PAIRING

shredded cabbage
sliced radishes
cotija
cilantro
diced onion
hot sauce
tortilla chips
limes

1 Cut one onion in half and cut the top off of the garlic bulb so it stays whole but the cloves are exposed. Place in a large pot with the pork, 6 bay leaves, a healthy dose of oregano and salt and pepper and just cover with water.

2 Bring to a boil and let simmer for about 45 minutes.

3 While the pork cooks, prep your chili base. Remove the seeds, stems and veins from your guajillos. Cut the tops off, cut in half, and discard the seeds and veins. Boil in water with more garlic cloves and half an onion.

4 Cook the chilis for about 10 minutes, then let rest to cool and absorb all that water. About 15 minutes.

5 Place the guajillos, garlic, onion, and about a cup of the liquid in a blender and blend until completely smooth.

6 Strain this heavenly base through a wire mesh strainer. Push the pulp through with the back of a spoon and discard the pulp.

7 Remove the garlic and onion from the pork and skim the fat off the top of the broth or you're going to have a greasy soup. Add the hominy, chili base, cumin, and salt and pepper to taste!

8 Simmer for about 30 minutes and then enjoy with all the garnishes and scoop that shit up with tortilla chips!

THE GARNISHES ARE THE CHERRY ON TOP, SO DON'T SLEEP ON THEM. I PREFER SHREDDED CABBAGE TO LETTUCE BECAUSE IT DOESN'T WILT AS FAST AND ADDS A LOVELY CRUNCH.

3 INGREDIENT TOMATO SOUP I MADE TASTE GOOD WITH 9 INGREDIENTS

3 ingredients my ass. If you can do 3, you can do 9 to make it worth eating. Pair this shit with a grilled cheese and call it a fucking day. This will also make you want a hand blender. Sorry.

ACTIVE 45 min **TOTAL** 3hr 30min **SERVES** 3 ungrateful kids, or 2 grateful adults

INGREDIENTS

- *1 28 oz can of whole tomatoes*
- *3 tablespoons of butter*
- *1/2 onion*
- *However many garlic cloves your heart tells you*
- *Heavy cream*
- *Chicken Broth*
- *Fresh basil, dried is fine I guess, but I'm judging*
- *Chili Powder*
- *Salt, to taste*

GARNISH/PAIRING

grilled cheese

1. Simmer the onion and garlic in butter for a few, then add the tomatoes and simmer for, I don't know, like 8 minutes?
2. Throw that shit in a blender and blend smooth while wondering why you STILL don't have a hand blender...
3. Return to pot with the rage of 1000 sons over having to clean your blender.
4. Add some chicken broth, heavy cream, basil, chili powder and salt. Simmer to let thicken.
5. Serve hot with a healthy side of contempt over the blender washing.

NEVER MET A BLENDER I DIDN'T HATE TO WASH.

Image | Sara Buckley

CHICKEN SOUP WITH NOODS

The only noods you'll ever see me post. My oldest considers any type of vegetable soup "peasant soup" but he sucks. I love a hot soup in the winter and this is easy as shit. Don't have noods on hand? Sub in potatoes or rice!

ACTIVE 45 min **TOTAL** 3hr 30min **SERVES** 6-8 Servings

INGREDIENTS

- *2 chicken breasts, diced*
- *1 pound egg noodles*
- *2 carrots, peeled and medium sliced*
- *1 celery stalk, medium sliced*
- *1/2 onion, diced*
- *1/2 head cabbage, medium sliced*
- *1 zucchini, medium sliced*
- *1 yellow squash, medium sliced*
- *8 cups chicken broth*
- *italian seasoning*
- *pepper*
- *garlic powder*
- *salt*

GARNISH/PAIRING

lemon
hot sauce
crackers or bread

1. Boil your chicken in slightly salted water until fully cooked. Remove and set aside.
2. Bring broth to a medium boil. Add seasonings, carrots, celery and onion. Cook for 5 minutes.
3. Add the egg noodles, zucchini, yellow squash and cabbage and cook until the noodles are soft.

That's it. Garnish it the fuck up and enjoy!

WARNING: YOUR KIDS MAY LOVE THIS OR THEY'LL ASK YOU IF THIS IS WHAT CHARLIE'S FAMILY HAD TO EAT IN WILLY WONKA BECAUSE THEY WERE SO POOR... LIKE MY SHITS DID.

Image | Sara Buckley

Image | Sara Buckley

CHINESE CHICKEN SALAD

My mom has been making this salad for 45 years. I've never seen or tasted anything like it anywhere else. It's a staple of my childhood and I bet my nostalgia you'll fucking love it.

ACTIVE 25 min **TOTAL** 25 min **SERVES** 6 if you feel like sharing

FOR THE SALAD

- *2 chicken breast, cooked and shredded*
- *1 head of lettuce, chopped into medium sized pieces*
- *3 green onions, chopped with tops*
- *2 avocados, diced*
- *2 celery stalks, sliced thin*
- *1/4 cup toasted seesame seeds*
- *fried rice sticks*

FOR THE DRESSING

- *1/4 cup vegetable oil*
- *1 1/2 teaspoons sesame oil*
- *3 tablespoons of white vinegar*
- *2 tablespoons sugar*
- *1 teaspoon salt*
- *1/2 teaspoon pepper*

GARNISH/PAIRING

white rice

1. Combine all salad ingredients in large bowl.
2. In separate bowl, combine sugar, vinegar, salt and pepper until the sugar is dissolved. Combine the oils and slowly add to the other ingredients while whisking rapidly.
3. Fry the rice sticks in hot oil. You'll know when the oil is hot enough by testing a small piece. If it puffs up immediately, it's ready.

Serve the salad on top of cooked white rice (can be hot or room temp) and top with rice sticks.

"YOU BETTER NOT BE TAKING THE CREDIT FOR MY SALAD IN YOUR COOKBOOK!" -MY MOM

Image | Bri Ramos

I WANT TO SAY BREAKFAST IS MY FAVORITE MEAL OF THE DAY, BUT I CAN'T DO THAT TO LUNCH AND DINNER.

BREAKFAST

Yes, cereal counts.

Image | Sara Buckley

Image | Sara Buckley

THE WORLD'S BEST BREAKFAST SANDWICH

"But eggs with peanut butter?" Yea bitch, that's what it says and it's fucking delicious. Unless you're allergic, don't say SHIT about the PB until you try it. This sandwich is ELITE and only peasants people disagree. The basil, PB, and peppadew combination is on another fucking level and you owe it to yourself to try it. Not to mention, serving this shit up to guests will feel FANCY AS FUCK.

ACTIVE 30 min **TOTAL** 40 min **SERVES** IT'S ONE SANDWICH, FIGURE OUT THE SERVINGS

INGREDIENTS

- *sourdough or regular English muffin*
- *breakfast sausage, ground*
- *egg*
- *avocado*
- *fresh basil*
- *sriracha*
- *peppadew slices*
- *peanut butter*
- *tomato, sliced*

GARNISH/PAIRING

bottomless mimosas

1. Hand form a thin sausage patty slightly larger than the muffin. The fat cooks out and shrinks your patty, and you're gonna want even ingredient distribution with this culinary triumph.
2. Cook through and toast the English muffin.
3. Scoot the sausage over and cook the egg to your liking, just try and keep it the size of the sausage patty. I love me some hot, runny yoke.
4. Spread peanut butter on one side of the muffin and avocado on the other.
5. Put a few slices of peppadew on the peanut butter and then a slice of heirloom tomato. I LOVE to cook mine in the sausage grease for a bit!
6. Put the sausage patty on top the tomato and then the egg. Drizzle sriracha on the avocado then stick 3-5 fresh basil leaves and put your gorgeous sandwich together!

YES, A FUCKING BOWL OF CEREAL

In case your mom guilt has told you otherwise, this is a perfectly acceptable breakfast. Serve with milk if you have enough, otherwise raw cereal is fine. Don't feel bad about "planning" for this meal either. You're probably cooking for people who eat their boogers. Add a banana or whatever if you feel bad, or some fruit snacks if you don't give a fuck. No kid ever ended up in therapy because mommy always had cereal on hand. Save the fancy shit for when you're actually hungry or a special Saturday when you're not on your period.

ACTIVE 1 min **TOTAL** 1 min 30 sec **SERVES** Your mental health

INGREDIENTS

- *cereal or crumbled up pop tarts*
- *milk (optional)*
- *side of fruit (laughably optional)*

GARNISH/PAIRING

extra sleep
mental health

1. Throw some cereal in a bowl or a cup.
2. Top with milk, maybe.
3. Offer fruit if you're feeling guilty even if they don't eat it. Hey, you offered.
4. Sit peacefully knowing your family is fed which is all any momma could ask for.

Image | Bri Ramos

CHILAQUILES DE RAMOS

Every time I post about chilaquiles, I get a few people telling me this is actually "migas". WELL WHY DON'T YOU TELL MY ENTIRE MEXICAN FAMILY THAT. Sorry, but we call this chilaquiles. Don't know what to tell you other then shut up and eat it. If you have a problem, take it up with my dad.

ACTIVE 30 min **TOTAL** like 45 min, I guess? **SERVES** Your whole stupid family

INGREDIENTS

- *12-ish corn tortillas, diced into 1" squares*
- *12 eggs*
- *vegetable oil, for frying*
- *onion, diced*
- *salsa*
- *salt and pepper*

shredded cheddar cheese (optional)

GARNISH/PAIRING

fuck "migas"
avocado
hot sauce

1. Heat oil and fry the tortillas until brown. Don't get impatient or your tortillas will be soggy and it'll be gross. You're basically aiming for chips here.
2. When the tortillas are almost done, add the onion and cook until translucent.
3. You can add some spices like cumin and paprika if you're feeling fancy.
4. Add eggs and scramble. There should be enough oil left from frying for the eggs not to stick, but add more if you need to.
5. Turn off the heat and add your salsa and cheese until melted. Season with salt and pepper.

THIS HAS A 100% SUCCESS RATE IN MY HOUSE.

Image | Sara Buckley

CHORIZO CON HEARTBURN

Ahhh, the desayuno of my childhood. Chorizo is a type of pork sausage, though it comes in beef too. This is the only way I eat chorizo: con huevos. It's cheap, fast, and actually only uses one pan. If you're over 30, it might give you heartburn.

ACTIVE 20 min **TOTAL** 21 min **SERVES** ???? fuckers

INGREDIENTS

- *1 package of chorizo*
- *15 eggs (I know that sounds like a lot but I have sons)*
- *cheese (optional)*

GARNISH/PAIRING

hot tortillas
avocado
sour cream
hot sauce
TUMS

1. Cook all the chorizo over medium heat. No need to add oil as there's plenty of fat in this. When the chorizo is fully cooked, it'll take on a deeper orange color and the rendered fat acts as lube for the eggs.
2. DO NOT SCRAMBLE YOUR EGGS FIRST. I promise you, just crack them all directly into the pan.
3. Mix the eggs well with the sausage and scramble until completely cooked. Add cheese if you want.

No need for silverware here, because your hot tortilla is your fork.

NOTHING CUTS DEEPER THAN SUDDENLY NEEDING A TUMS FOR A MEAL YOU'VE EATEN WITHOUT ISSUE SINCE CHILDHOOD.

Image | Sara Buckley

THESE-VEGETABLES-ARE-ABOUT-TO-GO-BAD BREAKFAST HASH

Image | Sara Buckley

My breakfast hash is basically a Frankenstein dish made up of whatever the fuck you already have. The ingredient list is a loose recommendation so no need to get hung up on it, but I used bacon and sweet potatoes this time. Fry this shit up fresh or use leftover veggies, add an egg and call it a morning. Leave out the meat for a vegetarian option and the egg/cheese for a vegan option.

ACTIVE 45 min **TOTAL** 3hr 30min **SERVES** IDK I'm over these recommeded serving sizes

INGREDIENTS

- *potatoes, peeled and diced*
- *bell peppers, diced*
- *onion, diced*
- *bacon, diced (or use sausage, ham, steak, whatever)*
- *oil, if you're not using bacon or sausage*
- *eggs*
- *paprika, chili powder, garlic powder, salt, pepper, italian seasoning*
- *cheese (optional)*

GARNISH/PAIRING

fresh basil
avocado
salsa
sour cream

1. Dice bacon and cook until crispy. Remove and place on paper towels to absorb the oil. If you're not using meat, skip to the potatoes and use vegetable oil.
2. Cook the potatoes in bacon grease until slightly browned. Add spices, peppers and onion. Cook until soft and tender like my lower stomach.
3. Turn off heat and add cheese and crispy bacon. Combine until cheese is melted, or leave it out, who cares.
4. Serve hot with a fried egg or scramble the eggs within the hash. You can also throw that shit in a tortilla for a bomb ass breakfast burrito.

A FRESH EGG ON OLD VEGETABLES = BREAKFAST

Image | Sara Buckley

CANNED BISCUITS AND SOUTHERN AF GRAVY

Feel free to look up some other homemade biscuits recipe to go with this, but I'll be using canned. The irony is that I'M TERRIFIED OF OPENING A CAN OF BISCUITS. If you're feeling SUPER fancy, include crispy breakfast potatoes but you'll have to Google that one too because I didn't write it out for this.

ACTIVE 30 min **TOTAL** 40 min **SERVES** Like 6 maybe?

INGREDIENTS

- *1 pound of pork sausage*
- *3 cups of milk*
- *1/3 cup of flour*
- *seasoning salt, cayenne pepper, black pepper*
- *canned biscuits, duh*

GARNISH/PAIRING

a fried egg
hot sauce

1 Over medium-high heat, brown your sausage breaking it up as you go. The crispier you get the sausage bits, the less soggy it'll be in the gravy.

2 When the sausage is browned to your heart's desire, make it rain on the meat. Stir so the flour can absorb all the sausage fat and cook for, eh, like 2-3 minutes. If you don't cook the flour all the way, it'll taste like raw flour, FYI.

3 Add the milk, one cup at a time, and whisk until smooth before adding another cup. Season with seasoning salt but taste as you go. The sausage itself is salty so chill the fuck out. Add the cayenne and black pepper according to your taste.

4 Cook the biscuits according to the nightmare-fuel packaging that's equivalent to an adult jack-in-the-box.

5 Serve the biscuits hot with a giant ladle full of gravy. I personally get turned on by topping with a fried egg and hot sauce. Don't kink shame me and enjoy!

FRIED CHICKEN AND TWAT WAFFLES

Your family puts the "twat" in Twat Waffles. I love making this, but honestly the amount of dirty dishes it creates is incorrigible. No worries, because anyone you serve this too will be willing to take care of the cleanup. Here's a waffles from scratch recipe, but unless it's Father's Day, feel free to use frozen.

ACTIVE 1 hr **TOTAL** 1 hr 30 min **SERVES** 4-6 twats

Image | Sara Buckley

CHICKEN

- *6 boneless, skinless chicken thighs trimmed of excess fat*
- *1.5 cups flour*
- *2 cups panko crumbs*
- *3 eggs, beaten*
- *vegetable oil*
- *paprika, onion powder, garlic powder, cayenne, basil, thyme, salt, pepper*

WAFFLES

- *2 cups flour*
- *1 Tbsp baking powder*
- *1 tsp kosher salt*
- *2 large eggs*
- *1 1/2 cups milk*
- *2/3 cup butter, melted*

CHICKEN SAUCE

- *1 stick butter*
- *1/4 cup honey*
- *hot sauce*

1 I use 3 pie dishes, but you can use whatever. In one, combine the flour and spices. In another, the eggs and lastly the Panko crumbs.

2 Dredge each chicken thigh in the flour and shake off the excess. Dip in the eggs, again letting any excess drip off. Cover in Panko.

3 Fry each thigh in about 3/4" of hot oil flipping after it's nice and brown on one side. Then continue to flip cooking about 1 minute on each side until cooked through. Let drip on a baking rack.

4 Heat the butter, honey, and hot sauce in the microwave and brush over the chicken.

5 Combine all the waffle ingredients. Spray your waffle maker with some nonstick shit and cook. If you don't have a waffle maker, I literally don't know what to tell you.

6 Serve with hot syrup and a chip on your shoulder for being fucking fabulous in the kitchen.

FANCY BREAKFAST FOODS ARE MY LOVE LANGUAGE.

Image | Sara Buckley

OLD ASS BANANAS IN BREAD FORM

Fuck regular banana bread. A cute mold and some chocolate chips though? Now that makes keeping black bananas in the back of my freezer for 6 months actually worth it.

ACTIVE 15 min **TOTAL** 6 mo 1 hr 4 min **SERVES** 1 person who loves banana bread

INGREDIENTS

- *1 teaspoon baking soda*
- *2 cups flour*
- *1/2 teaspoon salt*
- *3/4 teaspoon cinnamon*
- *1/2 cup butter, softened*
- *3/4 cup packed brown sugar*
- *2 large eggs, at room temperature*
- *4-5 brown-ass bananas, mashed*
- *1 teaspoon pure vanilla extract*
- *1/2 cup chocolate chips*
- *1/4 cup walnuts (optional)*

1. Preheat the oven to 350 and spray your adorable mold with non-stick spray. This mold is only $10 on Amazon!
2. Whisk the flour, baking soda, salt, and cinnamon together in a large bowl.
3. Beat the butter and brown sugar together on high speed with a hand mixer until smooth AF.
4. Add the eggs one at a time, beating well in between.
5. Add the mashed bananas and vanilla extract on medium speed until combined.
6. Slowly incorporate the dry ingredients into the wet ingredients until no flour remains. Do not over mix. Fold in the chocolate and nuts, if using.
7. Dump that shit into your cute ass mold (or use a 9x11 baking dish) and cook until a toothpick comes out clean, about 40 minutes.

SERVE THESE WITH WARM BUTTER. IT'S SO GOOD YOU'LL EAT THE WHOLE BATCH BY YOURSELF BECAUSE YOU DESERVE IT.

PUMPKIN SPICE "I'M BETTER THAN YOU" CINNAMON ROLLS

Is there a bigger breakfast flex than cinnamon rolls from scratch? No. These are definitely a labor of love, but worth the extra time if you ever find it.

ACTIVE 20 min **TOTAL** Feels like 10 hr **SERVES** 12-15 lucky sons of bitches

Image | Sara Buckley

ROLLS

- *4 to 4 1/4 cups all purpose flour*
- *1 package active dry yeast*
- *1/4 cup warm water*
- *3/4 cup pumpkin puree*
- *2 tablespoons pumpkin spice*
- *3/4 cup milk*
- *1/3 cup butter*
- *1/3 cup granulated sugar plus 1 teaspoon*
- *1/2 teaspoon salt*
- *2 eggs*

FILLING

- *2/3 cup dark brown sugar*
- *1 1/2 tablespoons ground cinnamon*
- *1/4 cup butter, softened*

FROSTING

- *4 ounces cream cheese, room temp*
- *1/4 cup powdered sugar*
- *2 tablespoons maple syrup or vanilla*
- *Pinch of salt*

1. Activate your yeast by combining the water (110°F), yeast and 1 teaspoon sugar in a small bowl. Let sit until foamy, about 10 minutes.
2. Combine milk, butter, pumpkin purée, the rest of the sugar, and salt in a small pot. Heat to 120-130°F. Yes, lots of temps, I realize.
3. Add 2 cups flour to your mixer and stretch because your shoulders are in for a workout.
4. Add the eggs, milk mixture and yeast mixture. Mix until combined.
5. Using a dough hook, add 1/2 cup of flour at a time to form a soft dough. It should pull away from the side of the bowl with ease when ready!
6. Remove dough from the bowl, make it rain flour on your counter and knead until dough is smooth and stretchy (like 6-7 mins).
7. Place in a greased bowl and cover with a towel for 1 hour or until it's doubled in size.
8. Roll dough into a 15" x 12" rectangle. Mix butter, cinnamon, and sugar for the filling then spread carefully over the dough.
9. Roll this beautiful dough baby into a the fattest white girl blunt you can imagine (long side first!).
10. Slice into 15 pieces and place in a 9x13 greased pan. Cover with a towel and allow them to rise (yes, again) for 40 minutes.
11. Preheat oven to 375°F and bake 20-25 minutes.
12. While the rolls are baking, combine cream cheese, butter, confectioners' sugar, vanilla or maple syrup, and salt with a mixer until nice and smooth. Allow rolls to cool for about 10-15 minutes and spread frosting on warms rolls!

THESE FUCKERS HAVE TO RISE FOR AWHILE, SO TIME THEM ACCORDINGLY.

I'M A DECENT COOK. BY "DECENT" I MEAN, THE FOOD IS GONNA TASTE GREAT BUT YOU'RE DEFINITELY BITING INTO A LEMON SEED.

Image | Bri Ramos

LUNCH

Who are we kidding, these could be dinners too.

Image | Sara Buckley

WE HAVE TACO BELL AT HOME CRUNCH WRAPS

PLEASE for the love of God, call these by their formal name after your kids tell you they love them. I guarantee they'll be furious at you for knocking it out of the fucking park while sticking it to them! Add egg and sub the ground beef for sausage for a breakfast version. If you don't have leftover taco meat on hand, cook the ground beef fresh with whatever seasonings you have on hand!

ACTIVE 25 min **TOTAL** 25min **SERVES** them right for asking to go to Taco Bell

INGREDIENTS

- *4 packs of ins, any 4 flour tortillas, burrito sized*
- *8 ounces ground beef, cooked (leftover taco meat works great too)*
- *4 tostada-shells*
- *1 cup bell peppers, diced*
- *1/4 onion, diced*
- *refried beans, canned or homemade*
- *cheddar cheese, shredded*
- *salt and pepper*
- *cooking spray*

GARNISH/PAIRING

sour cream
avocado
sriracha

1. Sauté the onion and peppers until fully cooked. Add the ground beef to heat (or sauté if cooking fresh).
2. Make a thin, tostada-shell sized layer in the middle of your tortilla. Top with the tostada shell.
3. Add the meat and pepper mixture. Top with cheese.
4. Fold the tortilla inward and overlap to cover the fillings. If the tortilla doesn't reach all the way, tear a piece of tortilla just big enough to fill the hole and fold away.
5. Spray a skillet with non-stick spray and place the crunch wrap folded side down first. Gently press down and flip once the tortilla is nicely browned. Repeat on the other side.

There's really no limit or rules when it comes to filling these. Use chicken, mashed black beans, pickled onions (recipe with White People Tacos), or whatever your heart tells you! As long as you have the tostada shell and brown the wrapped tortilla, it'll be a hit.

Image | Sara Buckley

EXTREME RAMEN MAKEOVER

While I did start this cookbook by telling you I have expensive taste(buds), my culinary vice is instant noodles. I fucking love ramen and fried noodles and could eat them every damn day. In an effort to make it feel more like a meal (and trick my family into loving this lipstick on a pig) I upgraded it. Take this shit from lunch to dinner by sautéing broccoli florets and shredded carrots with the chicken. BOOM! It's the food equivalent of transforming your daytime makeup into going out makeup.

ACTIVE 10 min **TOTAL** 15 min **SERVES** 4-6 Servings

INGREDIENTS

- *4 packs of instant noodles, any brand*
- *1 1/2 chicken breasts, diced*
- *2 eggs*
- *sesame oil*
- *sesame seeds, toasted*
- *1 shallot, diced*
- *ginger, fresh or powdered*
- *soy sauce*
- *pepper*

GARNISH/PAIRING

sliced green onion
sriracha

1. Cook the noodles according to the package directions but DO NOT ADD THE SEASONING PACKET. Strain noodles and set aside (yay a dirty dish for almost no reason, sorry).
2. Heat sesame oil in a skillet over medium high heat. Add the chicken and shallot and season with ginger and pepper. Sautée until chicken and onion are cooked through.
3. Add more sesame oil, the noodles, and a little soy sauce. Fry the noodles with the chicken and onions for a few minutes.
4. Make a hole in the middle of the pan, add more sesame oil, and crack both eggs into it. Cook for a few minutes before chopping up and mixing everything together.
5. Add 3 of the noodle seasoning packets and taste. If you want more flavor, add the 4th packet.
6. Garnish with green onion and a little sriracha if you're nasty.

Image | Sara Buckley

MOM'S IN A GOOD MOOD CHICKEN PHILLYS WITH SWEET POTATO FRIES

Image | Sara Buckley

Has your family been helping around the house lately? Listening to you the first time you say something? Highly doubt it, but whatever. Bless them with this lunch so you can guilt trip them into cleaning immediately after. My husband hates mushrooms, so they're not pictured here but he thinks bologna is edible so I'm putting them in the recipe anyways.

ACTIVE 30 min **TOTAL** 45 min **SERVES** 4-6 bad listeners

FOR THE PHILLYS

- *6 sub rolls*
- *2 chicken breast, diced*
- *1 green bell pepper, diced*
- *1/2 medium onion, diced*
- *3/4 cup mushrooms, sliced*
- *provolone cheese*
- *italian seasoning, garlic powder, salt, pepper*
- *vegetable or olive oil*

FOR THE FRIES

- *3 sweet potatoes, peeled and sliced in to fry shapes, lol (you can use russets too)*
- *salt, pepper, dried rosemary, garlic powder, onion powder*
- *vegetable oil for frying*

GARNISH/PAIRING

spicy brown mustard

PHILLYS

1. Heat oil in a skillet over medium high heat. Add the chicken and seasonings and brown for 3 minutes.
2. Add the veggies and cook until the peppers are soft. I prefer my bell peppers well done.
3. Toast the rolls, put the cheese on one side and spicy mustard on the other. Top with chicken and pepper mixture.

FRIES

1. Heat about 1/2" of oil in a pan until a potato immediately starts frying when placed in. Sacrifice a fry to test the heat.
2. Fry and flip as needed for about 10 minutes.
3. Toss with seasonings!

HOW *DARE* MY KIDS TELL ME THEY'RE HUNGRY AT 8PM AFTER I ALREADY SAID I WASN'T MAKING DINNER.

Image | Bri Ramos

IT'S DINNERTIME

sluts.

Image | Sara Buckley

CREAMY LEMON TIG O' BITTIES

Cutting these big, juicy breasts hotdog (not hamburger) not only reduces the cooking time, it increases the flavor coverage leading to a tastier dinner. This is a super simple main dish you probably already have the ingredients for and can pair with any carb and vegetables for a fully rounded meal.

ACTIVE 45 min **TOTAL** 3hr 30min **SERVES** 6-8 idiots

INGREDIENTS

- *3-4 chicken breasts, halved lengthwise*
- *2/3 cup heavy cream*
- *1/2-2/3 cups chicken broth*
- *1/4 onion, diced*
- *1 lemon, juice and zest*
- *Salt*
- *Pepper*
- *Garlic Powder*
- *Olive oil*

GARNISH/PAIRING

serve over rice or mashed potatoes
a vegetable, if necessary
fresh basil to flex on these hoes

1. Trim chicken of any fat or tendons. Cut in half lengthwise and pat dry.
2. Heat olive oil on medium-high and season one side of each breast with salt, pepper, and garlic powder.
3. When the oil is hot enough (but not smoking) lay seasoned side down. "Don't crowd the pan". Shyea ideally. It'll taste better if you don't, but if it's 7:45pm on a Wednesday and you're cooking for people who also eat boogers, just get the shit in there.
4. Season the other side and flip once browned.
5. Add a little oil, if needed, and the onion. Fit it around the chicken and let caramelize.
6. Squeeze half a lemon, and flip chicken.
7. When both side are nice and brown, add chicken broth, heavy cream, and the zest of half the lemon. Reduce heat and let reduce.
8. Sliced fresh basil is a nice touch, but extra AF and not necessary.

Image | Sara Buckley

ACTUAL ONE POT KIELBASA

Few things piss me off more than finding a "one pot" recipe that makes you dirty one or two extra dishes for 10 minutes because you cook everything separately. This ain't one of those. Literally one pot and lid is all you need. So easy, a husband could do it! This is a perfect, quick weeknight dinner that's ready in 45 minutes and is satisfying AF with whatever seasonings you have on hand!

ACTIVE 45 min **TOTAL** 3hr 30min **SERVES** Your whole stupid family

INGREDIENTS

- *1 pound of kielbasa sausage, sliced*
- *1.5-3 pounds red potatoes, quartered*
- *2 cans green beans, or fresh with some water*
- *1 head cabbage, cut into medium sized chucks*

GARNISH/PAIRING

salt and pepper
rolls, baguette, or your favorite bread with some butter

1. Canned vegetables gross me out, but they work great here. Open the cans of green beans and pour into your pot, liquid included. If using fresh, break green beans in half and add about a cup of water.
2. Top the green beans with an even layer of potatoes. If your potatoes are still pretty big when quartered, cut them a little smaller.
3. Cover potatoes with the cabbage. I like to lay the leaves flat and even.
4. Place sliced sausage on top of cabbage and bring liquid to a boil. The liquid from the green beans steams the potatoes in between the cabbage while heating the sausage.
5. Cover and cook on reduced heat for about 30 minutes!

THIS IS ONE OF THOSE "EVEN BETTER THE NEXT DAY" MEALS

Image | Sara Buckley

Image | Sara Buckley

NOT RED SAUCE AGAIN PASTA

Satisfying as fuck and done by the second "Mom, is it ready yet?" It's good on its own, but if you feel like blessing your family, throw in a bagged salad and garlic bread. Not homemade. I'm talking frozen food Texas Toast. It's a Wednesday. Not Christmas.

ACTIVE 45 min **TOTAL** 3hr 30min **SERVES** 6-8

INGREDIENTS

- *bell pepper, thinly sliced*
- *1 medium yellow bell pepper, thinly sliced*
- *1 medium orange bell pepper, thinly sliced*
- *1/2 onion, thinly sliced*
- *3 roma tomatoes*
- *1 pound penne pasta*
- *1 pound italian sausage*
- *1/2 stick of butter*
- *A fuck ton of garlic*
- *Olive oil*
- *Dried basil*
- *Paprika*
- *Red pepper flakes (optional)*
- *Salt and pepper*

GARNISH/PAIRING

parmesan
garlic bread
caesar salad

1. Cook pasta according to package directions. Reserve about 1 cup of pasta water.
2. Cook sausage in a large pan over medium heat.
3. Slice the bell peppers and onions into strips about the size of the pasta and cut up the tomatoes into chunks.
4. Add to sausage with a little olive oil.
5. Cook for, I don't know, like a few minutes? I like my peppers well-done.
6. Make a hole in the center, add the butter and a fuck ton of garlic. Let the garlic cook for 3-4 minutes until the butter is fully melted. Combine
7. Season to taste with: Dried Basil, Paprika, Garlic Salt, Pepper, and Red Pepper Flakes (if you want it spicy).
8. Add sausage and pepper mix to strained pasta. Mix well with some of the pasta water, if needed.
9. Top with parmesan and parsley (optional).

WHITE PEOPLE TACOS WITH PICKLED ONIONS

Image | Sara Buckley

This is another staple from my mom, but I add seasoning so I don't technically have to give her FULL credit. She can have like 85% credit.

ACTIVE 35 min **TOTAL** 45 min **SERVES** 4-6 people of any race

FOR THE TACOS

- *1 1/2 pounds ground beef*
- *1 medium onion, diced*
- *1 4oz can ortega chiles*
- *corn torillas*
- *your favorite cheese*
- *lettuce, shredded*
- *vegetable oil for frying*
- *salt, pepper, cumin, paprika, cayenne, oregano*

TACOS

1 Brown the ground beef in a skillet of medium high heat. When fully cooked, add the onion and Ortega chiles and cook until the onion is soft and beef is a bit crispy. Season with spices. In separate bowl, combine sugar, vinegar, salt and pepper until the sugar is dissolved. Combine the oils and slowly add to the other ingredients while whisking rapidly.

2 Heat oil in a pan on high heat, but don't let it start smoking. Fry one tortilla at a time for only about 5 seconds on each side. If the oil isn't hot enough, your tortillas will be soft and soggy. If you cook them for too long, they'll turn into tostadas.

3 Place tortillas on paper towels to absorb the excess oil.

4 Throw the beef, cheese, and lettuce in that bitch!

FOR THE PICKLED ONIONS

- *1 purple onion, thinly sliced*
- *1 1/2 cups white vinegar*
- *2 tablespoons white sugar*
- *oregano and red pepper flakes*

PICKLES ONIONS

1 Combine the vinegar, sugar and salt in a small pan and bring to a boil. Stir until the sugar and salt are completely dissolved.

2 Place the onions in a tupperware and pour the vinegar mixture . If it doesn't completely cover the onions, add a little water until it does.

3 Toss in the oregano and red pepper flakes.

4 Cover and let cool completely before eating. These are better the next day!

Image | Sara Buckley

COOL-MOM FROZEN PIZZA NIGHT

Let's be honest. Frozen pizza is a win all around because you don't have to cook shit and the kids love it. Upgrade pizza night by grabbing a couple different styles, a bagged salad, and of course ice cream because you're not a regular mom; you're a fucking cool mom who is tired and dad can throw pizza in the oven.

ACTIVE 5 min **TOTAL** 25 min **SERVES** 4-6 fucks you're related to

INGREDIENTS

- *whatever frozen pizza is on sale?*

GARNISH/PAIRING

bagged caesar salad
fresh basil for some greens so you don't feel bad
red pepper flakes

1. Ask the kids what they want for dinner at around 1pm.
2. When they request pizza, say no and keep suggesting the worst fucking dinner ideas. Like everything they hate.
3. Fried tofu sticks with ketchup?
4. How about sardines with lemon on top saltines? (Legit my dad's favorite snack, barf)
5. Or tell them they can have cereal.
6. At around 6pm, get those pizzas in the oven and prep the salad. What's that? The kids don't want salad?
7. Bribe them to eat it by telling them about the ice cream.

POUR YOURSELF A DRINK AND GO TAKE A BATH WHILE CATCHING UP ON YOUR FAVORITE SHOW.

THERE'S PLENTY OF LEFTOVERS FEND FOR YOURSELF

I know this sounds like a joke, but I am not fucking kidding. If you're cooking lunch and/or dinner everyday (shit, even every other day) eventually there will be enough leftovers to feed everyone at least one more time. Seriously, plan for this shit. Don't let those leftovers go bad and REMEMBER: your family can eat it or go fuck themselves.

ACTIVE 0 min **TOTALLY** Guilt Free **SERVES** Them right for talking to you when there's leftovers

INGREDIENTS

- *All that shit you've already cooked*

GARNISH/PAIRING

peace of mind

1. Ummm, this isn't a recipe?
2. Yes the fuck it is. A recipe for dinner success when you're juggling housework, kids in school, extra curricular activities, a marriage, mental health, and life goals.
3. So take this lovely reminder to heart and stop throwing food away!

Image | Bri Ramos

Image | Sara Buckley

BONUS RECIPE!

SALMON THAT TASTES GOOD

Is it just me, or is salmon way more fucking expensive these days? Chicken, pork, and beef get old QUICK when you cook a lot. Throwing some fish in the mix can be a welcomed change, *if* you can afford it.

ACTIVE 30 min **TOTAL** 45 min **SERVES** Like 6 maybe?

INGREDIENTS

- *enough salmon to feed your hoard*
- *dry or fresh minced ginger*
- *chili powder*
- *salt*
- *pepper*
- *honey*
- *soy sauce*
- *lime juice*
- *broccoli, cut into florets*
- *carrots, sliced*
- *sesame oil*
- *olive oil*

GARNISH/PAIRING

cooked white rice
sliced scallions

1. If your salmon isn't already cut into individual servings, do that first. Leave the skin on for now! Pat it all down with a paper towel so you get a nice carmelized outside.
2. Combine the ginger, chili powder, salt, and pepper to make a rub and coat the salmon. If you like to eat the skin, rub that too. If you prefer it skinless, save the rub for after you remove.
3. Heat sesame oil over medium-high and place the fish skin sidedown. Cook for about 5 minutes or until the skin is very crispy. If you're removing it, flip and gently pull. If it doesn't release easily, let it cook a little longer. Season under the skin with remaining rub.
4. Flip your filets over and turn until cooked through. I prefer my fish a little dry, so I cook it LONG.
5. Combine honey, soy sauce, and lime juice for the glaze. Pour over salmon and turn the heat down until the sauce thickens.
6. Toss your carrots and broccoli with some olive oil, salt and pepper and bake on a cookie sheet at 400 degrees for 16-18 minutes.
7. Throw all this shit on top of some white rice!

WHY IS IT ALWAYS "WHAT'S FOR DINNER?" AND NEVER "YAY, CEREAL AGAIN!"

Image | Bri Ramos

DESSERT + COCKTAILS

IF they deserve it.

Image | Sara Buckley

DRINK ME LIKE ONE OF YOUR FRENCH GIRLS

A better cocktail doesn't exist! If you're a Lemon Drop fan, you'll love this too. Fresh squeezed lemon juice and homemade simple syrup, aren't COMPLETELY necessary, but you'll definitely be able to taste the difference. Simple syrup is essentially the liquid form of sugar. It's difficult to fuck up this easy of a recipe, but know if you "cook" it too long, you'll have candy so pay attention.

ACTIVE 5 min **TOTAL** 6 min **SERVES** 1

INGREDIENTS

- *1 oz of your fave gin*
- *3/4 oz fresh lemon juice*
- *1/2 oz simple syrup*
- *3oz of your fave champagne*

SIMPLE SYRUP

- *1 cup white sugar*
- *1 cup water*

GARNISH/PAIRING

curly lemon rind

SIMPLE SYRUP

1. Combine the water and sugar in a pot.
2. While stirring, heat until the sugar dissolves. DO NOT OVER COOK.
3. Chill before compiling your cocktail!

FRENCH 75

1. If you chill everything beforehand, you don't have to do all that shaking over ice bullshit, but obviously you don't want to drink this warm.
2. Combine gin, lemon juice, and syrup and mix well.
3. Top with your champs.
4. Instantly feel more refined even if you do black out later because these are delicious.

BONUS RECIPE!

Image | Sara Buckley

PASTRY NINJA STARS

These are fun for dessert, an app, or breakfast because why not? Easy as shit, not expensive, look way more advanced than I'm capable of and my kids loved them. No, they don't love everything I cook either! A tasty variation to the fruit is some jam and if you're feeling extra slutty, throw some nuts on it too.

ACTIVE 45 min **TOTAL** 3hr 30min **SERVES** 6-8

INGREDIENTS

- *2 sheets of puff pastry, thawed*
- *8 oz cream cheese, softened*
- *1/3 cup powdered sugar*
- *1 teaspoon vanilla extract*
- *2 tablespoons of lemon juice*
- *pinch of salt*
- *flour, so your shit doesn't stick to the counter*
- *raspberries and blueberries*

GARNISH/PAIRING

powdered sugar
lemon zest

1. Preheat your oven to 400 degrees.
2. Let your puff pastry thaw, flour your counter, and open that shit up flat. Cut into 9 equal squares.
3. Cut a slit from each corner toward the middle leaving about 1.5" uncut for the filling.
4. Combine the cream cheese, powdered sugar, lemon juice, vanilla extract, and pinch of salt in a bowl.
5. Spoon about 1 tablespoon of filling into the center of the ninja star. Take one corner and fold it over, pressing into the bottom of the section next to it. Don't cover up the cream cheese. It doesn't matter which direction you fold as long as you fold them all the same!
6. Place your a few berries on top the cream cheese center and bake for about 18 minutes until the pastry has a beautiful tan.
7. Dust with a little powdered sugar and lemon zest if YA NASTY.

Image | Sara Buckley

MY MEXICAN GRANDMA DIDN'T CARE THAT I GOT PREGNANT YOUNG, BUT SHE'S ROLLING IN HER GRAVE WATCHING ME POUR COLD WATER ON HER HOT SKILLET.

Image | Bri Ramos

Image | Bri Ramos

HOW TO RUIN CAST IRON

IT'S ACTUALLY PRETTY EASY...

MYTH: CAST IRON IS INDESTRUCTIBLE

First of all, have you ever met me? I can literally ruin anything. When my grandma passed away, the only thing of hers I wanted was the cast iron skillet. Had I ever cooked with cast iron before? No. But did I at least know how to care for it? Also no. I think I just figured that if she cooked with it and I knew how to cook her recipes, I'd be fine. I WAS VERY WRONG.

HOW TO DESTROY IT

If you're looking for how to season, store, cook, and care for your pretentious-ass skillet, Google it. You can't teach what you don't know, so here's how I ruined mine.

1. Don't season it, because you don't even know what the fuck that means and then wonder why every food sticks to it.

2. Wash by hand with soapy water or throw it in the dishwasher with a chemical filled detergent pod to expedite the destruction.

3. Cook acidic foods for hours on end, like tomato sauce.

4. Because the sound it makes is so much fun and the steam gives you a desperately needed facial, be sure to pour COLD water into the middle of your HOT pan. Over a short period of time, this will inevitably warp the bottom (if not CRACK it) so it doesn't lay flat or cook evenly.

It's THAT simple! Good luck.

SPICE GUIDE + CONVERSION CHARTS

Image | Bri Ramos

Image | Sara Buckley

SPICE GUIDE

I *hate* pre-made rubs, but will agree they have their purpose. I'm not burning through half a jar of 7 spices for rib racks, ya feel me? In my opinion, a lot of pre-made rubs have a weird after taste. Building your own seasonings with individual spices gives you a lot more freedom and control over the flavors. A well stocked spice cabinet is a great foundation for pulling a meal out of your ass at any time. And let's be honest, that's the majority of the time. Here's is what I always keep on hand!

MUST HAVES

- BASIL
- BAY LEAF
- BLACK PEPPER
- CAYENNE
- CHILI POWDER
- CILANTRO
- CUMIN
- DRY MUSTARD
- GARLIC POWDER
- GINGER
- ITALIAN SEASONING
- KOSHER SALT
- ONION POWDER
- OREGANO
- PAPRIKA
- PARSLEY
- PINK SALT
- RED PEPPER FLAKES
- ROSEMARY
- SAGE
- THYME
- TURMERIC

OILS

- OLIVE OIL
- SESAME OIL
- VEGETABLE OIL

ACCEPTABLE RUBS

- RIB RUB
- CHINESE 5-SPICE
- TAJIN
- CREOLE SEASONING

Image | Sara Buckley

CONVERSION CHARTS

VOLUMES

FLUID OUNCES

1 oz	2 tablespoons	8oz	1 cup
2oz	1/4 cup	12oz	1.5 cups
4oz	1/2 cup	16oz	2 cups (or 1 pint)
6oz	3/4 cup	32oz	4 cups (or 1 quart)

WEIGHTS

OUNCES	GRAMS
1	25
2	50
3	75
4	110
5	150
6	175
7	200
8	225
9	250
10	275
11	315
12	350
13	365
14	400
15	425
16	450

TEMPERATURE

°C	°F
140	275
150	300
160	325
180	350
190	375
200	400
210	425
220	450
240	475
260	500

Image | Bri Ramos

WELCOME TO MOTHERHOOD. "EASY DINNER RECIPES" WILL BE YOUR TOP GOOGLE SEARCH FOR THE NEXT DECADE OR SO.

Image | Bri Ramos

THANK YOU!

I know I talk a lot of shit, but seriously THANK YOU!

While I'm terrible at expressing any emotion other than sarcasm, I will do my best to ariculate this level of gratitude. Your support not only vindicates all the dinners I've ruined over the years...it's shown me I have so much more to offer than I ever expected. It's given me a confidence boost I didn't think I needed.

To me, this isn't *just* a cookbook. It's an entire new chapter of my life. It's a way to combine my passions for food, comedy, and my family. I consider cooking for others a very pure form of love, and with this book I can love all fucking over!

Thank you to my husband who's been overwhelmingly supportive in this new venture. Thank you to my kids, who've honored me with their sophisticated palates even though chicken nuggets are A LOT cheaper than the lamb they request.

Follow me on Instagram, Facebook, Twitter, and TikTok: @NotTheWorstMom.
Keep an eye out, because this is just my *first* cookbook.